Broken to Mend

Poems

Broken to Mend

Poems

Ricardo Tane Ward-Ramirez

ALAMO BAY PRESS
SEADRIFT•AUSTIN

Copyright © 2024 by Ricardo Tane Ward-Ramirez

All rights reserved. No part of this book may be reproduced in any form without permission in writing from the publisher, except by a reviewer who may quote brief passages in a review.

Cover Art: Annalise Gratovitch

Book Design by ABP

Alamo Bay Press

Lowell Mick White, Editor
Diane Wilson, Activist

Pamela Booton, Director
825 W 11th St Ste 114
Austin, Texas 78701
pam@alamobaypress.com
www.alamobaypress.com

ISBN: 978-1-943306-25-1
LCCN: 2024940163

-For Ryk-

The world was created through many stages. In one instant good vanquished evil and it was sent fleeing throughout the lower world. Still it finds and infects us. Still it leads us down a crooked path that ends at the sea. There will you wash in the cold waters where sharks and whales breed. There you will cry for the ones you lost and the wrongs you committed. There you will see just how big the world is—so much larger than good and evil. Yet the pulsing tide that tickles your toes begins at the greatest depths and reaches for the old woman in the moon who still loves us in each and every stage of her transformation.

Contents

Cracks	1
Sunders	21
Fetters	47
Stiches	71
About this Book	95
Acknowledgements	97
About Ricardo Tane Ward-Ramirez	99

Broken to Mend

Cracks

To sit in sunlight and dream of the candle
Neither warms the body nor enlightens the spirit
Never look beyond what you can see
Instead feel the serpent in your leg
Reaching downwards into the solid world
A reflection is always less real than its source

Mi Diosito

This morning I made coffee for God
I made him breakfast of vegetables and eggs
I washed God's body and hair
I poured love into each act
Love that is reserved for divinity

Today I danced with God
Moving his body in as elegant forms as he would let me
Today was a day of worship
I cared all the while for God
Until with a prayer I laid him to bed.

Trees

I don't know why the trees forgave me
After I had chopped so many of their kind down.
But they did.

I don't know why the grass still smiled
When I crushed it underfoot.

I cannot tell you why the sun still rose
After I had cursed existence.

But then I remembered that we are all bound by love.
What then could I do but plant trees and dance upon the grass?

What could I do but give thanks each day for the rising sun
And remember to forgive all those who do me wrong?

Ricardo Tane Ward-Ramirez

Sideways Healing

My father, who lives inside my right knee
Has discouraged my television career
Closure is critical for ghosts

I apologize over and over for practice
In case I run into people we knew

An angel gave me a feather from her wing
The wind moves freely expelling the blockage
I receive council from rejuvenated joints

Acceptance

In walking the maze we become lost
And yet the center still beckons us beyond the dark passageways
The sun destroys the morning star each day
But it is still up to you to get up early and pray beforehand
All beauty is inevitably lost to time
But this does not keep you from dancing throughout life

All I ever wanted was peace in a world of war
And healing in a world of wounds
Yet stillness does not calm the wind
The rabbit does not reason with the wolf
He must become cunning

Pain is the parent of healing
War stewards peace and suffering conceives contentment
Until we accept the rules of the game we will be disqualified
And remain ineligible for the prize
The perfect circle is facilitated by the square lines of the grid

Altar

Your ancestors are cheering you on from the altar
As you navigate the vertical path and fall yet again before yourself
It is the moment that the dead long for—the moment to be alive
You are here as an extension of every root on your family tree
Numerous shoots cling to the dark ground of the past
Each a story that searches for healing inside the stalk that reaches for light

As you muster the strength to bifurcate another branch
You catch a glance of your future reflected in your past
You sit among blessed things in the place you have created
Arise and meet the sky

Memories

I remember when you left me
Alone upon the sand
I remember when you let me know
That I was not a man

I remember when you left me
So long ago in time
I remember feeling weak
How you left me all the time

I remember when you left me
To cry alone in shame
I remember this so well
Because it happened every day

I remember when you left me
That sad day that you died
I remember then you let me
Let you leave me one more time

Ricardo Tane Ward-Ramirez

Wholeness

One missing string on one violin can muffle an orchestra
One quivering hand can weaken an army
One missed step shifts the entire dance outside of its delicate
    pattern
One deficient protein strand will cripple the development of
    an organism.

The pressure upon each cell to function
is the same force that maintains an entire Earth
The destiny fulfilled by each particle of light
is the very function of the sun
that sustains every living creature we know.

Can we truly dance offbeat when we surrender?
Or is it an evil impulse that moves us away from our creator?

We are in perfect pitch when we let go
And we stray from the chorus when we grip too tightly
to our separation.

María

Every time I am reborn my mother is in the dream
Each time I find something that changes my life
It is my mother giving birth once again

To learn through intelligence is fleeting
As our cloud mind merely grasps at existence
Always gazing too far afield in fantasy

But to learn in the body is to verify Truth by living
To enact one's own creation is a knowing all in itself
It is a lesson that traps the mind of God

To live is the fantasy of the unborn
To be whole is the dream of the imp
So we grow to our greater form of knowing

How far we have come
How much farther we have yet to go
Knowing we will go together

This is the inheritance of our Mother
And all she teaches us

Ricardo Tane Ward-Ramirez

Learn to Act

You act out your script within this world
You are the will of the gods
You are their folly
And you are their reward
You are the creation that gives them meaning
You are their creator as flesh

Missteps are myths of warning
Triumphs are eternal odes of praise
To the creator of great and small
Of God and man and our shared destiny
So act according to the text
Stop stepping on everyone else's lines

The Heron

There was an instant when the world was created
When light shone for the first time
A gentle sun peeked out upon the horizon
Glowing pink with promise of all that would come

The first sunrise is within all of us
As we were created then
This is the place of the heron
The temple of Bennu, the land of Aztlan

The light reflecting upon the water
Illuminates the blessing that we are here—alive
The stilted legs and piercing beak demonstrate mastery
over the underworld—without pride. With Reverence

Our origin is light kissing darkness softly
A still pond of reeds cradles the chorus of genesis
All that will ever be is within the wise countenance of a bird
Our divinity was always within us

Relief of Stress

My shoulders are stiff with the stress that my brother felt at the time of his suicide for feeling that my father never loved him.
I try to massage it out with prayer.

My teeth clench from the hand of great-grandfather against grandmother's face.
I reach for forgiveness inside my decanter heart—a salve to soothe the soreness from generations of built up resentment that became propaganda to justify my family's behavior.

I stretch into my body and feel deeper still into the goddess who sits beneath my center. It is calm in the rose colored light.
A little frog shelters beneath the cactus-covered hill. The mountain conjures us here to slay demons with our interlocking rhythms.
My sea washes into a vast silver basin when crescendo reaches peak.

There are no shoulders amongst the waves.
We are beyond fluid when we are light.
There are no jaws within the fire.
The portal in my rib cage folds us together into a mirror of red.
We heal when we open our heart.
We succeed each time we relax.

Prayer

I give thanks at the spring for the creation of this beautiful world
And I give thanks that I am here
I ask the crayfish to carry the prayer directly to God
He returns with a tiny piece of earth in his claws
All it takes to create a universe is a speck of dust
And the divine

I remember a man who had been addled by disease
With drought stricken fields and hungry children
Yet he still tilled the soil
His smile shone like the sun
Relentless in channeling blessings
As to be alive—in any state—is a condition worthy of praise

I lost part of myself when I gained new perspective
I let go of purpose when it stagnated
I hardened like stone and yet the winds chiseled me into a new form
A statue that stares at the stars
A cornerstone for the holy temple

I found myself in a constellation
Each person in my life fitted into place
Spokes in my spinning center
What could I do but send the wheel racing towards our collective destiny?
How else could I steady the hub of my world
But for gratitude that we are alive
Here upon this beautiful Earth?

Ricardo Tane Ward-Ramirez

Compost

The ground is softest where the most has died
Where the most prayers have been laid down
As living is a prayer
And dying is a prayer

Thorns ensnare the fool who forgets his enemy
Wisdom tends the broken branches fallen after a storm
And clears a path for others
Take off your shoes so that you can hear the stones

Don't distinguish yourself from others
but focus only on similarities
Then you will be taken on a blessed journey
Full of friends and allies

Sink your toes into the soft ground
There you will feel your ancestors
And recognize your similarities
Then your prayer will be completed
And your path will be clear

Yorkshire

I no longer wander amongst the dales
But now lay stones for the path
So that my great-grandchildren will find their way home

I no longer seek upon this world
But now lay the stones of home
To which my children will one day return

I plant my staff upon the hill
So that in 100 years they may sit therein and eat cherries

And I walk with my own legs
So that I heal this body for my son to see himself within me

I am whole upon this path of stone, within this heated home
Underneath the abundant sweetness that feeds me

I am within the Center that time turns around
And my grandfather's eyes look into me as clearly as my grandsons

Ricardo Tane Ward-Ramirez

Symbols

A strange mark appears upon the land
Ominous
Like a rune of unknown origin
Burning raised in stone

We had to work with what we were given
We had to heal what was wounded
No general sense of purpose will fix our specific problems
No dogma will answer our questions

When mystery decides to assert itself
Over the false world that we use as shelter
Then there is little we can do but marvel
At our smallness

When a hurricane destroys your home
There is nothing to do but rebuild it
No amount of prayer will hammer in the nails

The curse upon your soul courts the work of angels
No ointment will salve the depths of those wounds
No dictionary will decipher the arcane script written on your
    back

Beyond Grief

How many have held my grief with ears and skin?
How many have I carried upon my back?
We heal each other as we walk the winding path
We summon from within shelter from war and storms
We grow into great beasts to fend off evil
We become fires to warm weary bones
Upon an altar we sit as candles welcoming the dead
And upon mutual thrones do we bow in reverence
When we recognize God in each other's eyes.

Sunders

There are no right answers in heartbreak
There is no closure in closings
An opening lies in healing
Closure lies in silence

Divergent paths are the branches of our tree
We grow; we open; we remain silent
And still there are no right answers
Only growth

Freedom

I am fire. Like the fire I am free
To burn all I touch to ashes
I am free to be tamed into utility
I am an agent of creation
And destruction
I am free

God granted me freedom today
Indeed he has done so every day since I was born
So have I been burdened to live and die
By my own hands
So have I nurtured life as water
Free to take infinite forms
Free to flow and saddled with being needed
I am free

I danced
But then others stopped to watch
I move without number or letter—only wind
I am free from grasp and cage
I am free to wander and be lost
I am free to be lonely and even alone
Passing through this place like a mortal
I am trapped in a temporal stasis
Awaiting the beyond

I grow and am grown from
I am ground
I am center
I am roots
I generate radius and sprout trunk
To form, I am a ghost
I begin in ether
I am mind

Today I was granted the freedom to live
And so it is each day that I visit this place
Never complete
Always in motion
I am free

Ley Lines

I bit a raspberry hanging in midair and it splattered blood on the invisible threads of web holding this world together

We expose the ley lines that order our deeper existence when we give a little sacrifice

The truth is written clearly enough for anyone to read, but only sounds right when it is spoken in your voice

There is something waiting for you on the other side of the veil
It will take more than patience to achieve your goals

You will be required to find a rhythm from the other side that you can dance to
Then must you study the sacred steps

When you find your body moving beyond your known abilities
Then rest assured that the web exposed beneath reality is your road

It is time to make an offering to the god of the forest
It is time to train your arms and legs

The truth is written clearly enough for anyone to read, but only sounds right when it is called out by a hawk or as it shines through a window in the morning...
or as it moves through the delicate body of a dancer

Incision

On the other side of the incision I am whole
On the other side of the half moon I am growing
Down river I can hear the prayers of those who were once my kin
On the other side of the knife—the cold stone only receives

I feel you letting go and prospects appear on my horizon
The seven stages of craziness are low lying foothills
From the peaks of madness I have summited
Up high I am a cold wind
The birds read me like the daily paper
The clouds ride my currents like turtles
Errant prayers heal strangers
No one sings for me while I sit here alone

Through this land—a mother—I have had many brothers
Through this fire—a father—I have had many sisters
Upon this medicine road
What is new is neutral
It is a peace swept over by wind and fire
No thorns or twisted stalks
Just soft beds of clovers and flowers

On the other side of gestation I am a spark
The fusion of light and matter
On the other side of life with its habits and dramas
I await birth and death from a quiet place within me

Ricardo Tane Ward-Ramirez

My palate crumbles in my mouth releasing pent up
 resentment
I glue my skull back together with salt and concentration
I plant myself deep with my soul and water my ground from
 heavy clouds
I radiate down upon my Earth from my Sun
I illuminate my own darkness

A vulture comes in the back way and picks me apart upon the
 highway
I am liberated from the ego and the animal and I return to the
 mind
Beyond the vultures that circle in the sky

Sedentary

I will build myself up from the heron
I will live from the frozen pit of death that is within me

I will heal from the small piece of sickness
That I keep tucked into my liver
From the hollow reeds of the marsh will I build my kingdom
From my wanderings shall I settle
In my stillness will I find the movement that animates me

Alone, but for the reflection upon the water
Looking down from the sky behind me
I rise, striking down the ego
The spear is a beak that cuts the glass
From this sacrifice am I born
From this sunrise will I stand as a heron
From this prayer will I heal

Gifts

I am grateful for the steep incline
It reminds me that I am strong

So long I prayed for sore muscles
Not for weariness but conditioning

So long I courted closure
Not to forget but to evolve

So long I sought answers
Not for fortune but for purpose

I asked life for the honor to live within her
So now I give thanks

Not for grandeur but gradient
Not to harvest the fruit but to plow the ground

I give thanks
Not for the sake of doing
but being

New Mouth

As my broken mouth heals
From telling too many lies
I learn how to tell the Truth
I learn to accept

I learn to eat again
In an unfamiliar way
And must assess every item
That passes through these sacred lips and teeth

I learn to speak again and each word emitted is strange
A foreign accent binds my diction into an unknown voice
And every sentence I speak haunts me
Like a scripture carved on an ancient temple wall

I must learn to kiss again
My hungry tongue can no longer satiate his infant lust
But must receive like an old worm
Living deep beneath the Earth

I learn to rest—my jaw tenses from holding too many feelings
I give them expression in order to validate feelings in this
    world
In hearts of other men who clench their mandibles
With fear of the policemen inside their heads

Ricardo Tane Ward-Ramirez

And so my mouth learns to bite again
The teeth of the wolf have been broken like his spirit
And they remain jagged, so my new mouth bites with
    precision
the doubt in my head, and kills it.
Now I can speak the Truth
With my new mouth

That I am free

Blood

I bit my own face
I was bitten back

I vanquished my enemy
I have been vanquished by the victorious within

I am sick—so that I may heal in good health
And to know in my heart that it is I—not someone else—who is healing

I needed to taste my own blood again.

Ricardo Tane Ward-Ramirez

Emission

The ashen aura burns off like morning clouds
And I shine white again
The grey sticks to ghosts
Both living and dead

A light brighter than fire
Emits a cleaning agent from your spirit
As you connect to others
You all see more clearly now that you breathe 'out' instead of 'in'
The song in your dream lulls to rest the anger in your heart
Now you can feel the pendulum within you pushing and pulling
As intuition upon your muscles

Trust yourself—don't hold back your ability to heal
Let gratitude flow from you at all times
But only receive what you discern useful
Sustain what you have learned
Your hurt will no longer hurt others
Because now you can tend to their spines

Now you can sweep clean the earth
Now you are on the other side of the river

SLC

In an earlier developmental stage
I staggered from tragedy to tragedy
In an uncoordinated trajectory
That bounced hard against the steel wall of lockers
And alcoholism and derangement

I bounced straight up
I went so high that I never stopped climbing
I had bigger fish to fry than childhood trauma
I was "saving the world"
I had no reason to linger on the force that threw me
On the concrete blacktop like a rubber ball

I went to places of knowledge that explained everything
I sailed to distant shores where I gained perspective
I follied and fought my way through experience
I became a powerful man
Because I had escaped the place I now sit within

It feels strange to be back in Salt Lake City

Ricardo Tane Ward-Ramirez

Distance

Out past the last outpost
In the emotional wilderness
I am beyond all science and reason
Confusion is cold and dark
On the other side is mystery
And her consort—unexpected beauty

I am awed at my adaptation
To successive worst-case scenarios
Driving me away from civilization
Keeping me out past the lights and sounds of cities
And healthy human relationships
Now I am amongst the wolves

Trees offer shelter to my discomfort
The wind speaks directly to my solitude
Distant peaks beckon my anger
To gather my bones and climb high into the cliffs

Courting misfortune frees us from feeling like we don't belong
Finding purpose sometimes means skirting death
There is a long way down on either side of the mountain
An agonizing and terrifying fall
Or an agile decent with staff in hand
Carrying the laws of our people

Shoulders

To be real...
Isn't that all any of us want?
Can I just cry, man?

Can I not pretend to be ok
For an instant
And just be as I am?

Can we be whole here
Or do we keep each other from being seen
Because we are accustomed to looking away
From the Truth?

Being

I am
I became
And I was

I was fire
I was power
I was knowledge
But unknown

I am stone
And I am tower
I am matter
Only where the light is shone

I am river
And I am vessel
I am alive
And still I'm dying

I am tree
And I am chisel
A creator and still
Destroying

I am, I acknowledge
All these things
That live and breathe
Within me

I am flower
And I am taste
I am, I was
I will be

Mirrors

When I can remember to—I look the apparitions directly in the eyes
That way I can tell which ones are angelic and which ones demonic
I tell them all that I love them—it attracts the good and repels the evil

When in my haziest state I spit venom
At a version of myself I project onto my enemies
I must remember to look them in the eyes

We have no reason to invite sin into our lives as an excuse for divine drama
It finds us without need for justifications

Perhaps we are the evil part of divinity
But divine nonetheless

Beluga

I have fought evil in my life
And it has fought back
I have won some and have been worn down by some
The road is long in our dual relentlessness

I picked through carpet for glass
That had been shattered for 34 years
And still cuts my feet

I find an alley for a hit of something sweet
Just to be loved for a little while

I remember something the beluga whale said
Except it came in another language
That spoke to the heart

"Let go" she said "of all that is weighing you down.
There is work to do." The beluga told me
We have fought evil together ever since

Ricardo Tane Ward-Ramirez

Six AM

Victory comes at 6 AM
Seize this world by the devil and wring its neck
The warrior succumbs to his own power
Surrender to yourself
As you rise beyond what you were last night
And the night before

Rebirth happens in the morning
And with proper training comes every morning
When you are ready to take responsibility for your life
It begins at 6 AM
Then you will see the responsibility
That you have in the world
In the soft light of dawn

Only then will you remember past lives and grieve your defects
Only then will you see forward to your day
And the day after
Only then will you be co-creator of your future
You will be a warrior
Starting at 6 AM
And every succeeding hour

Halfway

In a not so distant future I look back upon this moment
With immense gratitude for all that life has given me
And all I have done with it

They say that you inherit your life halfway
And the other half is up to you to create
So after a setback or seven I am ready to comply with my mission

In this incubation I have learned to breathe and listen to my blood
I have learned to love and to lust and to trust my body
To know what it needs and wants

I have learned to communicate a little better than before
So have I become more human

Struggling to communicate and to give and receive love
Only makes me more like everyone else

I thrive in this defensive posture
Like a turtle
Like a stone

Gratitude

I am grateful
I am gratitude

I am love
Recognizing itself in creation

I am resplendent
My heart blossoms with the intensity of the sun
That pulls all flowers into the world

I am life
For a moment in time, I am an entire life

I am grateful

Fetters

To evade the lesson upon your path will lead you off course
To deny growth perverts the world
So allow yourself to decay
Return to the earth
Die upon the hill
So you may be reborn

Falling Completely Apart

When I worked hard to hide the truth
For fear of hurting others
I only spread lies

When I sheltered the vulnerable from danger
I incubated cowardice within them

When I stifled my strength of force
With a hope of bringing peace
I demonstrated weakness
And so war came to my doorstep

Everything I gave of myself was so another would be strong
    and free
I see a mirror of confusion as to how I could be so wrong
And every temple I pray to toppled like flimsy sticks
Stacked by a foolish kid

My anger has been hidden
And it is no wonder that you would stoke the flame
Can I marvel at my happenstance?
Or must I admit that I knew this day would come
When I would only have my own two legs to stand on?

Recognition

You know what they say
Shame recognize shame
That is how I cracked the mystery of my father
Long after his death

I came to know this man by denying him within me
So did I deny the source of anguish from which I would never
 escape
Until I found so many missteps in becoming who I was
Just like in the fables, fate unfolded

Some things in this world are dark
Fate is of the most sinister pitches
The clarity of complete blindness
Is the god of the wrathful

I remember hiding for days because of what I had done
I knew that no matter what I did, it didn't matter
I had no power to change anything
There was no washing away who I was

I cannot say whether it was my father or I
Who hid and cried and pretended to be strong
I cannot say if it was he or I who resented his father
And slowly over time learned to forgive and love him

Ricardo Tane Ward-Ramirez

Apology

I'm sorry for that time I broke your face
And that time I choked you out
I'm sorry for my fantasies
I am sorry for my wicked wants
I am no longer sorry for my feelings
But must dig at the roots to expel them

I'm sorry I cheated on you and made you wait
I'm sorry I put up with it when it was my turn to be
    embarrassed
And I knew I deserved it
I can only be accountable to myself now
I'm sorry you're so hurt
And I'm sorry that you can't say sorry

I'm sorry I killed you
And your family
And all of your people
When my lust for power was too great to contain
I'm sorry I spread lies to justify this genocide
I'm sorry for all I have built from your bones
My house, my bank, my armies
I'm sorry I burned this world to ashes

I'm sorry
It was shame

Okay

I bear down and get pummeled again
Storm surges are caused by family and friends
The angel who refuses to pull me from the water is my only ally
My boots are made of invisible lead

In the dark sludge I can almost hide
But I am a red newt popping from the mud like fire
My tears are for human beings who were kept in zoos one hundred years ago
My rage is for their captors whose books I was told to read
To earn letters that allow me entrance to different spaces of racism
It's a shame how mediocrity has allowed this whole mess to continue on for so long

A gale of winds brings another round of self-doubting down upon my head
I struggle to collect myself long enough to stand up when I need to
While my own knock me down

It's a bit harder to feel ok when it's not ok
And that's ok, I guess
For now

Ricardo Tane Ward-Ramirez

Neutrality

They took the middle ground
Neither standing for Truth nor Lies
But in between
They sided neither with justice nor treachery
But stood in a void between them
And sucked us all down into a cold objectivity
Where we became stale and orderly
No chaos cut us down
Nor triumph raised us to glory
We were destroyed by not taking sides
The courageous and coward are one
And morals have lost all meaning
We are safe now
It has never been more dangerous

No Time for Games

It amazes me that evil so easily creeps back into my head
Even after all that healing
Doubt is his pawn lurking in the small spaces in my habits
Second-guessing is his knight leaping over my defenses
Dwelling becomes hypnosis
Hate is the primal scream that slept inside me all along
I breathe fire at the imaginary foes
All with my face

All I ask anyone is that they allow me my grief
Otherwise I will explode
Mostly they hide in bunkers of numbness
And pull my pin with absence of sympathy
I move as close to the queen as I can
The bishop with my head moves diagonally from heart to heart
I leave a mess

Inheritance

I cannot stop the patricide, my son
But I can teach you about death

As you walk into the world—as a man—you will walk alone
No matter the thousands of women who carry you
From womb to tit to economic and social system
No matter how many people you manage to love or destroy
Upon this green earth, you will be alone.

What a shame it all was
How we disappointed each other
Even after all these long cycles

"Look, Dad, I turned out just like you."
"Sorry, Son."

Severed Hand

When I lost my hand in battle I gained new purpose
Unable to point, I held; unable to reign, I led;
No longer able to count, I imagined I was whole

I become not incomplete, but remade
Not missing nor seeking
Not still yet an anchor for movement

When I lost my hand in battle I became the scale
I bring balance because I know imbalance

To commit atrocity on the battlefield
Made me an expert on morality and compassion
As I once enforced their submission to vulgar power
When I lost my battle I became the enemy of corruption
When I gave my sacrifice
I realized the divine within me

Ricardo Tane Ward-Ramirez

Entrance

I wore God as a yellow feather in my cap
I earned it when I rose and fell
I touched another sky
One that sank beneath my peaks

I smelled another flower
From one that grew before me
I felt freedom in my bones
That chilled me like the wind
And through all of this I was weary
Where would my head rest when I had no strength?

So far above the clouds there was no ground to rest upon
Would my love rebound back to me if I kissed into a stellar void?
I floated adrift with no salt in my body
A flat note played on an angel's harp
I looked for a ladder to climb back down to Earth

Suddenly my foot stuck to a string
A thread that led to a web ensnared me
I found my self bound inside a map of the universe
Woven by God—This time she was a spider
Not a bird—and she spun me up and ate me
And shit me into more web
So now I am sticky and I catch lost souls
Who float upon the ether
I transmute my relatives back to Source

When I fell from grace
I had to go in through the side entrance
Just to peek at the throne
Upon which I will never sit.

Escape

To escape is to close the mind
Allow nothing to enter or exit
This is the chamber of pleasure
In which you hide when you are lost
And fear the predator at your heels

Escape like the wise hermit in his tower
Escape like a fool falling down a manhole
Escape to the silent cloister in your soul
Gather strength there
Where the lion cannot find you

Frolic in the meadow on the other side of fear
This is your liberation
When you emerge from the place of nothing in your mind
You enter the world of everything outside of you
You are free now to escape into light

Curse

No matter how much I loved him
I could not keep my father's curse from my son
The story had to be told
Ashes got hotter as the sun burned on

We are all one story
Told over and over
God going through a midlife crisis
Again and again

The Wound

I'm not used to feeling confused
Or losing my head
When the heart breaks—as was in my case—the brain shuts
    down to mend it
Movement comes from the wound

I'm not used to lashing out
With the evil strength within me
When the world shatters—as was in my case—
And the psyche retracts back into the primitive mind
To escape the carnage—until there is only reaction
A scared animal moves from the wound

I'm unaccustomed to withholding love
Or being needy rather than needed
And yet when one is exhausted in the spirit—as was in my
    case—
The energy is drained away from strength
A vampire within starts to suck out secrets
Revealing the wounds from which we move

I am unaccustomed to being so hurt
And so I am—broken—and in search of healing
Still I wait—as not to move from the pain
I call upon the four winds to move me
None of this is unique or new
It is love.

Dirt

My grip weakened from squeezing too tightly
I let her leave to grow on her own
Though I was heartbroken—it was for love

I stumbled across a field of littered feelings
And wondered how people still manage without them
I mined in my own psyche for reason
Artifacts emerge from the core—broken and buried and
Molded into little burdens

I found insecurities from when I had yet to learn
I found pieces of despair from before I learned hope
I found self-loathing left over from a time before the
    realization
Not only that I am a sacred being, but a human being
Deserving of love and destined to give it

And now with my knowledge—the confidence of shovel in
    hand
I still find myself blindsided by betrayal
I am moved to a state of madness where I grab her wrists and
    scream
Because I feel I have lost her love
I am confused. I am weak and I am dangerous

Ricardo Tane Ward-Ramirez

I receive back everything I gave, including the pain
This is the love I was promised in the primeval state of
    awakening
This is the life I cobbled together from discarded stones
I thrash in the dirt unable to grip a trowel
Jagged bits of remorse poke at my soft underbelly
Where my daughter used to snuggle me
When I pretended to be strong

Aspen

I do not feel clean or dirty
But I feel alive
All that is precious to me is vulnerable
It is time to make decisions
Creation is guide—manifestation is reality
I can be with myself now—human and holy
I can be with this world

I can heal in this world
I can grow
An aspen sapling connected to rhizome ancestors
I am alive now—as I have always been
And I am beyond life now
Neither clean nor dirty

Ricardo Tane Ward-Ramirez

Re-Spawn

I found religion in the woods
God smiled down upon me
I received a blessing and a message

We transform by night
Through acts of love and rebellion
We claim our power under the superior planets

I un-hex an old spell that I had cast against me
I ask the Lord to carry one more
He puts it on my auntie's tab

I find four thousand years ago an ancestor laid upon a slab
And the stone remains worn by rain but functional
The sacrifices we gave over the years will come back to us
The forest unfurls thick ferns of unanswered prayers
Awaiting an age of silver to re-spawn

Teacher

When confusion comes from a wounded place
I struggle to offer tenderness
Too squeamish in my own uncertainty
I put my finger in the incision
Infecting others from my specialized cultivation of germs

I went under the knife of my teacher
When they cut me open from within
A guru in their own confusion
And rebellion

Instead of lungs I am now only air
Falling into an empty space
That calls out from the other side of form

Life is culled into existence by knowing
Not knowing
Then knowing again.

The Fire

All the anger I had for you is gone. I put it in the fire.
The sorrow I had left over was taken the same way.
I laid all my troubles down and watched them burn away.

And so I reached for yours—I felt your anger back at me—
And I put it in the fire. Deep inside I found your sorrow
And it was taken the same way.

I reached further into you, to Dad and Grandma
To the bully who punched you in the second grade
I laid it all down.

I reached for those who had done wrong
To the people who had done you wrong
And put their troubles in the fire too
All was taken.

I reached for war and conquest
Back 500 years
And all the anger and resentment
Left over from such carnage
I laid it down
Laid it down
Laid it down

Everything was taken by the fire.

Stiches

A warm light holds us in place
Giving strength to our arms and eyes
Never before have we risen so high
Not like eagles, but like clouds
We illuminate a new dawn
As ancients reborn anew

Permission

I ask the riptide if I may slip beyond this world into heaven
She answers "no" and I wash to shore and remain to suffer

I ask the reptile if he might grant me his coldness of heart
He answers "no" and I remain to love

I ask the tree if I too can grow roots to hide myself deep in the Earth
"Only if you grow tall enough to shelter those around you," he replies
I say "yes" and slip into the waters of heaven. I become a mighty Baobab
Reptiles seek refuge in the ground amongst my roots

Isolation

Sometimes I wish they had faces
And not just masks
I cannot strike or kiss such plastic replicas
That tokenize humanity piece by piece
Until we become data

I identify with the ghost
Never Pac-Man
Which not only makes me bad at games
But afraid of banks
And stupid rules

Small acts of treachery are always offshoots of deeper roots
When the child notices the sacred tree is really a strangler vine
They see their father at fault for their own vulnerability
How can I protect my son when I carry his wounds?
How can I heal my people when we tumble under the same
    crashing waves?

If I could connect to the humanity of the executioner
the moment before he lifts the axe, we might just escape
but he wears a hood to conceal his features
Evil has no face but our own
nor an enemy as potent as our execution

Ricardo Tane Ward-Ramirez

Whale

There is a whale who sings to me
The faint tone of her song slackens the grief
She is calm as she rises beneath me demonstrating the
    immensity
Of beast and sea—and darkness
When she lifts me from the water I become a chord between
    ocean and sky
Between grief and love
I balance on her snout like a showman
I possess her power to navigate the depths of all that I feel

Bifurcation

The narrative bifurcates and creates two realities
One in her psyche and the other in mine

I find my mythology full of forces to overcome
They are ghosts from my past and monsters upon my horizon
They are my hesitation and doubt
I am called towards the journey

In her story a castle has crumbled
With her own house burning and tumbled from the tower
I stand as the destroyer amongst the rubble
Until I disappear into the forest

There is no easy peace as there is no easy truth
There are two people who struggle to communicate
They tried and failed to relate and feel safe
In the reasoning warmth of arms

It was two people suffocating
in the comfort of their bed
Not because there was not love
But because love had never fulfilled its own destiny

There is no single story but there is Truth
There is no myth without calamity
Just as I cannot escape the fact that I am a villain
In at least a few quantum realities

Untethered

Becoming free, becoming whole
Becoming untethered from control

Becoming a fractal replication
Of a greater manifestation

No longer knowable or wise
Now knowledge and wisdom

No longer man, now in this becoming
Neither an individual nor a part of anything

Now you are everything—beginning and end
Sun and flower and the dirt that you tend

Become the connection between all that is and will be
Away from control—whole and free

The Other Side

After my fear was spent
I approximated bravery

After I spread all my irrational anger and insecurities
All that remained was an empty ego
Almost Zen in its openness

After my fear was spent
I had no more lies to hide behind
I had no clouds of confusion granting me cover

After years of twisting in and out of responsibility
And running from fate
I had nothing left to whisk me away

I remained to look my enemy in the eye
The mirror showed a fearless beast
One who devoured a coward over long years of chasing him down

After the fear was spent
All that was left was bravery
An acceptance of fate and a commitment to character
All that was left was me

Courtship

Do I court the devil with my abstinence
And the angel with my passion?
Am I a pendulum ordering the heavens with my swing?

Am I flesh that attracts flesh or spirit that attracts spirit?
Who is the host and who is the guest here—my body or my soul?
And who has the upper hand?

Perhaps there is no difference in how we pray and how we dance
Perhaps sin is not learning a lesson and blessings slap us steady
Perhaps I should know better by now how to walk along this path

Confession

In an effort to clean up my mess
I looked deeply inside myself
I saw a blindfold knitted long ago by an unsafe feeling
I took it off carefully after much struggle
And the light that entered my memory
Illuminated more than I had bargained for

I see clearly that I have been wrong more times than I can count
And yet the feeling could not have been more real
I felt attacked each time despite the intention of the alleged attacker
When they hurt me I hurt them back

Now in the clear light of day
I feel my confusion rattling against me—not malice
I can hear in my memory other stories I had not heard before
Misunderstandings and stumbles of communication
That I did not respond to with a hand but a fist
I did not lift with kind words but cut down with bitterness

I am sorry everyone—I have a lot of unlearning to do
Perhaps we can go back to before I was warped
To a place where I am free to scream like a baby at the first signs of danger
So you could hold me in your arms and I could coo an apology
And you could cradle me in a forgiving embrace

Ricardo Tane Ward-Ramirez

Duty

This land is thirsty and you are water
So be deep and full

Your people are sick and you are medicine
Be kind and forgiving

Spirits wait to continue the cycle
Be present and listen

Do not resist the flow of the river
Float like a log

Do not rebel against life
Or death

Proposal

I wonder how it would feel to wake up in that distant
    dimension
Where the forests are happy and the stars are visible
But I will have to settle for my dreams
And your arms

Connections are universes when we share
They are prisons when we act like guards
A chisel was baked into a cake to facilitate my escape
It took the form of the hearts I had to break
Just to reach your embrace

And what do you hide inside your universe?
Is it intended to break my teeth or chains?
Do you stoke my dreams with the shine of your stars?
Do you tap into the fire that once burned down these old
    forests?
Do you hold in your heart a future where I am happy and
    whole?
Will you bring me peace?

I ask because birds carried your seeds from afar
and sought roots where soil welcomed you in.
But to sprout, the hard shell must crack under flame
and my flint has often lost its spark

Can I break your chains with my Truth?
Can we sit in silence with the cruelty all around us?
Can we be free together in each other's arms?
Can we be the universe?

Ricardo Tane Ward-Ramirez

Texas

In this time of sacrifice
You will be the sacred calf

And you will be the knife that slices its throat
You will be the blood that is lifeforce and sacrament

You will kill the cow within you as you kill the greater cow
The cattle industry that destroys the natural world

Jerky for generations will be slaughtered en masse
To emancipate the soil from hooves and fences

Cedar will be fuel for ten thousand fires and
The people will pray in ten thousand lodges

The cities will empty into liberated land
Bison will return to the southern plains

The future will birth itself as a new world
We are midwives to our healing

Good things will come to us
But first you must make the sacrifice

Greeting

"Hi, how are you?"
"I am healing"
I become the stars each night

"What have you been up to?"
"I have been feeling"
The sun in every drop of light

"Its good to see you"
"It's been so long"
Watching unraveling fate

"So, you know, let's go
It is time now"
The other side patiently waits

"When is it going down?"
"Forever, and so let us link arms
And learn from each other"

Greet each person upon your path
With God on your lips
And each God on your path with evasive action
Take each lesson as merely math
Not personally attacked in misalignment
Welcome the spirits to this world
Like a womb receives a soul

The Loom

Sister holds me
Pushing me through anguish
She has walked this road much longer than I

We are linked, I realize, not like a chain
But like fabric—Wound is loom
Into which beautiful colored threads are fed

The cloth that emerges from our steady hands and hearts
Can cover the cold and warm the children
That sit within us

The designs we weave channeled
From a place beneath this world where we are all born
Without time we become like spirits

The glass of water on the altar is always full
Even when it is empty
For the ancestors satiation is eternal
But thirst remains in time

We do not fear the future
We are just learning patience
A tiny spider shoots off her web and floats into the distance
We still circle the sun.

The Sea and the Moon

    Truth—as spoken by the word of God—is in all things
    Yet you need to learn to listen—pause a moment and look
    Make no excuses and see what is there
    Eternity is unkind and inevitable

    All that is sings in a chorus, as the conductor stands silently before us
    One hand grasps a staff to command—the other holds us steady
    So we may hear the entire orchestra and not only our own wavering voices

    We are the sea and not the fish, but God is the moon
    As surely as the moon is also the fish
    As surely as your own wavering voice
    Is the very Truth you must pause to hear

Ricardo Tane Ward-Ramirez

Beyond Dreams

She finally came back to the hand in the jar
And knew she had to swallow it

The moon offers us transformation
The sun never abandons us
The painful road is already your path
So why not enjoy the sharp stones on your soles
Instead of getting lost in the brambles and thorns

The scroll knows your destiny
But its runes are your senses
And the parchment is your skin
The medicine you take is what keeps you from getting well
Letting go will be hard

No combthrough is sufficient
Train yourself to be crazy
Like a monk who studies a century
To learn the simple truth that he is human
So when he dies at 104 years old
He will rest enough for his mother and father

So will you let go and rest
Coax your brother out from behind the glass
You are already a master
Your pupils await

Saturn Returns Once Again

It is not arrogance within me that repels you
It is shame—sometimes they look the same
I judge no one below me
For I have been at the bottom

I looked up and I saw you there above me
I see you from an angle you will never view
You are complete to me in a way that you will never know
No matter who you become in the next stage of your life

I know an old woman whom I speak to when I am disguised
    as a tree
She wears a pendant of Saturn around her neck
And speaks to birds
Long ago she forgave her father

She sees now this storm eye of transition
She is free from the threat of patriarchy
Her grandmothers' wisdom has returned
She mends my broken wrist
with the tender understanding
of an ancestor receiving a glass of water on an altar

I remember—although not clearly—offering her fruit from my
    branches
I remember her fastening a broom from my fallen limb
I remember how she holds the handle
When she sweeps the house clean

Ricardo Tane Ward-Ramirez

When victory is no longer an option
There is still redemption

In the end I will summit this peak
No matter how many times I stray from the path

We all return to zero
By slowly letting go of one

About *Broken to Mend*

Broken to Mend was written as a healing practice. All of the wounds explored in these pages—the cracks, sunders, fetters, and stiches needed to be cleaned and dressed by the alchemy of words. Each poem put one piece of me back together from the many falls I have taken. It is my hope that others may find pieces of their own selves here in these pages as well.

Acknowledgements

This book is possible because of my mother María as she birthed and raised me and is always my first reader. Thanks to my publisher Pam Booton at Alamo Bay Press. Thanks to my wife Paola and my children: Belen, Facundo and Tanito. I also extend immense gratitude for my second reader, utmost supporter of my written work and dear friend Grace Morris.

About Ricardo Tane Ward Ramirez

Ricardo Tane Ward-Ramirez PhD writes poetry, nonfiction and fiction focused on mythology, mysticism, social justice and indigenous knowledge. Tane's first book *The Maze of Creation: An Alchemist's Guide to the Center* was published in 2019 on Little Crow Press. He earned his PhD in Anthropology in 2014 from The University of Texas. Tane plays music, performs theatre and works as a consultant in Austin, Texas where he lives with his wife, children and dogs.

www.ingramcontent.com/pod-product-compliance
Lightning Source LLC
Chambersburg PA
CBHW060534080526
44586CB00012B/730